All Aboard the
LONDON
BUS

'To Don, in celebration of our wonderful years in London'
D.H.

First published in Great Britain in 2017 by Frances Lincoln Children's Books,
74–77 White Lion Street, London N1 9PF
QuartoKnows.com
Visit our blogs at QuartoKnows.com

Text copyright © Patricia Toht 2017
Illustrations copyright © Sam Usher 2017

The right of Patricia Toht and Sam Usher to be identified as the author and illustrator
respectively of this work has been asserted by them in accordance with the
Copyright, Designs and Patents Act, 1988 (United Kingdom).

A catalogue record for this book is available from the British Library.

ISBN 978-1-84780-857-8

Illustrated in watercolour

Designed by Andrew Watson • Edited by Katie Cotton

Printed in China

1 3 5 7 9 8 6 4 2

All Aboard the
LONDON
BUS

Written by **Patricia Toht**
Illustrated by **Sam Usher**

Frances Lincoln
Children's Books

Come!

Board the double-decker bus

and see the London sights with us.

At any time, hop off.

Explore!

Then climb back on and ride some more.

For better views, climb up the stairs –

the city views are great from there.

Here's your map and city guide.

Settle back. Enjoy the ride.

Buenos días!

Bonjour!

Hello!

Guten Tag!

Nǐ hǎo!

Let's go!

CHANGING OF THE GUARD

I'm standing at the Palace and

I'm trying very hard

to stretch my neck enough to see

the Changing of the Guard.

Jumps and tiptoes just don't work.

I hope some people shift.

I'm way too short to see – could someone

please give me a lift?

  I can hear a rum-pum-pum –

  Steady thumping of a drum,

  Trills and tweets and toots of brass.

  If only I could see them pass!

ARRGHH!

I'm standing at the Palace.

Being patient is so hard.

Hey! Someone moved and…

  Oh!

   I SEE!

The Changing of the Guard!

LOOK UP!
...LADY'S CHAPEL
High above this holy space
the ceiling's carved like loops of lace.
A stony net of whorls and waves,
brimming full with prayers and praise.

LOOK AROUND! …POET'S CORNER

Groups of tourists stop and stare,
reading tombstones, unaware
around them writers' spirits lurk,
busy editing their work:
nouns to tweak and verbs to mend,
and NEVER happy with 'The End'.

**LOOK DOWN… GRAVE OF
THE UNKNOWN WARRIOR**

Gravestone,
shiny as tears,
rimmed with blood-red poppies.
Below lies a lone soldier, name
unknown.

· NEXT STOP ·
BIG BEN

A BELL NAMED BEN

At rest inside the golden tower,

a giant bell awaits the hour.

Tick-TOCK, tick-TOCK. The clock marks time.

Ding-DONG, ding-DONG. The small bells chime.

Then, at the hour, a hammer pounds.

The bell lets loose with wondrous sounds

that ring and echo, loud and long.

The song of Big Ben –

BONNNG!

BONNNG!

BONNNG!

EYE-CATCHING

A bracelet that hangs off the arm of the Thames,
its pods, filled with people, all dangle like gems.
The glass capsules glimmer and coloured lights burn,
splintering sparkles with every turn.

The river rises, the river falls. Winding its way past government halls, under broad bridges, by market stalls.

TUMBLING THAMES

Its bubbling blends with chimes from St Paul's. Splashing and lapping against Tower walls, the river rises. The river falls.

SEEK AND FIND

10 pigeons scatter as toddlers run and play.

9 ladies chatter on their way to a café.

8 performers pose as grateful tourists clap.

7 workers doze and take a lunchtime nap.

6 dogs on leads get tangled in a knot.

5 students squeeze in a phone-box photo shot.

4 lions laze as exploring children climb.

3 statues gaze and politely pass the time.

2 fountains burst in a bubbly waterfall.

1 Lord Nelson watches high above it all.

SPEAKERS' CORNER

Speakers on boxes,
and speakers on chairs.
Some raise a fist or
wave arms in the air.
All have a message
they'd like you to hear,
so join with the people
gathering near.
Sometimes a heckler
shouts from the crowd,
when more add their voices,
things can get **LOUD!**
So, come hear the Hyde Park
cacophony –
opinions are plenty,
the speech is free.

• NEXT STOP •
HYDE PARK CORNER

COCKFOSTERS   2 MINS

THE TUBE
Glowing light.
Gust of wind.
Rumble.
Screeeeeech!
Train pulls in.
Cram aboard.
Jam-packed space.
Back-to-back
and face-to-face.
'Mind the gap!'
'Clear the doors!'
Hisssss. Ka-thunk!
Off once more.
Wheels squeal,
rails spark,
swerve and curve
in the dark.
Whip! Zip!
Station-bound,
riding on
The Underground.

· NEXT STOP ·
PICCADILLY CIRCUS

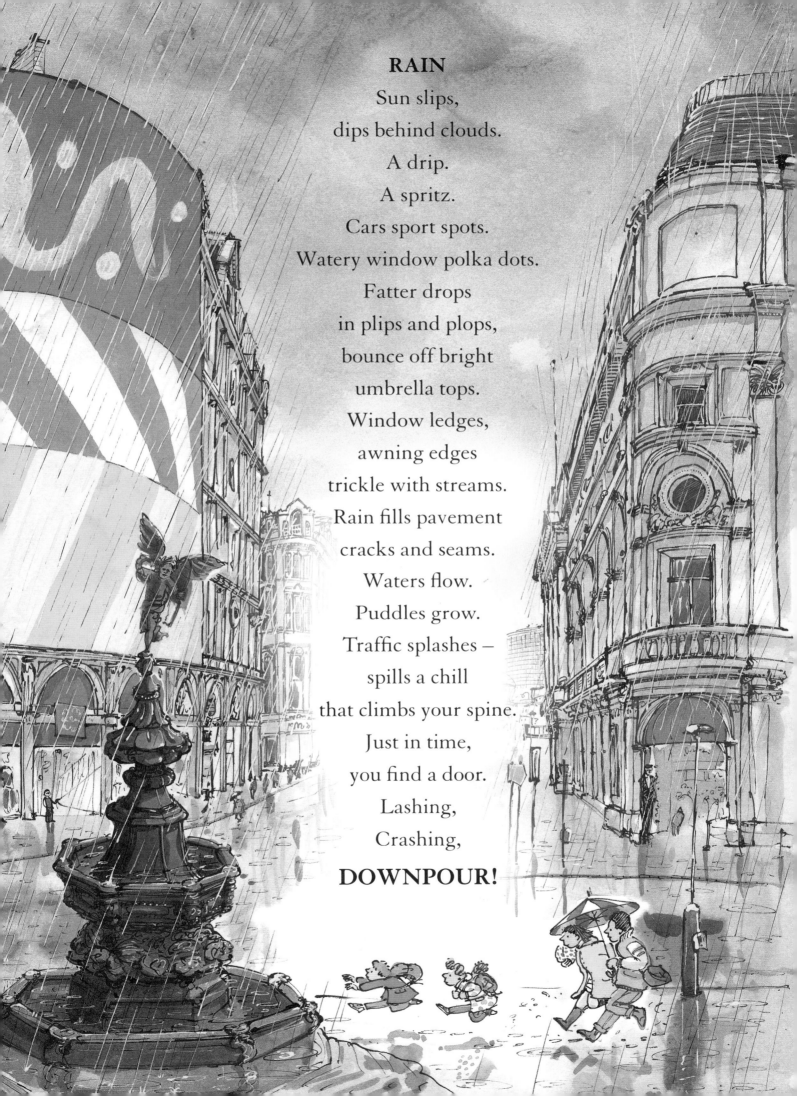

RAIN

Sun slips,
dips behind clouds.
A drip.
A spritz.
Cars sport spots.
Watery window polka dots.
Fatter drops
in plips and plops,
bounce off bright
umbrella tops.
Window ledges,
awning edges
trickle with streams.
Rain fills pavement
cracks and seams.
Waters flow.
Puddles grow.
Traffic splashes –
spills a chill
that climbs your spine.
Just in time,
you find a door.
Lashing,
Crashing,
DOWNPOUR!

TEATIME

Let's stop for tea,
just you and me.
We'll dry our cold, wet feet.

Here's a spot.
The tea is hot.
The scones and jam are sweet.

Rain may spill
and wind may chill,
but we'll just say 'Pooh-pooh!'

Ignore the storm.
We're dry and warm,
enjoying tea for two.

EXPLORE A STORE
Let's go explore
this splendid store.
We'll buy a little treat.

Climb moving stairs
past cuddly bears,
and sets of drums to beat.

Sleek cars to race.
Big balls to chase.
And piles of
puzzles, too.

Aha! This floor
has DINOSAURS –
the perfect thing for you!

· NEXT STOP ·
THE BRITISH MUSEUM

A GALLERY OF HAIKU
Beyond the black gates,
treasure troves to navigate.
Surprises await!

A CAT MUMMY

Cat, wrapped in repose,
cloth crisscrossed from paws to nose.
Endless, wide-eyed doze.

THE CLOCK SHIP

Galleon of gold,
bells and cannons in its hold.
Bong! Bang! Time is told.

ROSETTA STONE

Egyptian decree,
hieroglyphs, a mystery.
This stone is the key.

GREEK VASE

Stuck inside this case,
barefoot runners in a race.
Never-ending chase.

CATHEDRAL RISING

Wind-whipped,

flames ripped through

wood,

pitch,

hay –

anything in their way.

A firestorm raged.

Too fierce for a bucket brigade.

Stones burst like grenades.

Air thick with heat,

beat back crowds

choking on smoke.

Days later, the City woke
to cinders.
From embers and ashes,
a Cathedral rose.
Growing,
year after year,
stone on stone,
pale white walls
and elegant dome.
Pure.
Proud.
Immense.
Wren's finest of all –
St Paul's.

TATE MODERN

What's modern art?
Not 'by-the-book'.
It's fresh and quirky –
take a look.

Painted cartoon fighter planes,
WHAAM – a crash and burst of flames.

That's art!

Blurry murals fill a room,
blocks of red, black and maroon.

That's art!

A can-you-spot-the-difference game;
fifty portraits, none the same.

That's art!

Shapes and balls in balanced stance.
A breeze begins a bouncy dance.

That's art!

Now – let your imagination flow.
Plant ideas, watch them grow.
Do your part –

MAKE ART!

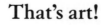

A GROUNDLING AT THE GLOBE

Buy your ticket (just five pounds),
join the crowd within the grounds.
Perch up front so you can lean,
stand in back, or in between.
If it's sunny, you may sweat;
If it rains, you may get wet.
Here's the hero. Give a cheer!
There's the villain. Shout and jeer!
Can you stand through one whole play?
Hold on 'til the last 'Hurray!'
Be a groundling in the yard –
'Give your hands!'
Applaud the Bard!

REGISTERING MY COMPLAINT

Dear Visitor,
I grow weary of being
called by the wrong name.
I tell you, 'London Bridge'
and I are NOT the same!
Years ago dismantled, he
was shipped across the sea.

And, without a doubt,
he's not as GLORIOUS
as me.
I decorate the city like a
fancy wedding cake,
while unadorned,
he plainly spans
an Arizona lake.

Sincerely,
Tower Bridge

TOWER of LONDON

GOODNIGHT, TOWER

The sky grows dark. The hour's late.
It's time to lock up every gate.
Goodnight moat and massive walls,
chapels, prisons, stony halls.
Goodnight dungeon deep below
and jagged gate where waters flow.
Jewel House is safe and sound –
goodnight sceptres, orbs and crowns.

Ravens, close your beady eyes,
dream sweet dreams until you rise.
Yeoman Warder, rest your head.
Your family's snugly tucked in bed.
A bugle sounds. A final bell.
The Tower's locked
and all is well.

Find out more about London!

Buckingham Palace/The Changing of the Guard

Buckingham Palace is the main London home of the Royal Family. It has 775 rooms, including 240 bedrooms and 78 bathrooms, plus its own chapel, swimming pool, cinema and post office! The Changing of the Guard takes place in front of the Palace every morning from April to July, and alternating days in other months. A new group of soldiers (the New Guard) marches in to take over from those who have been on duty (the Old Guard). With horses, bands and ballyhoo, they swap places.

Westminster Abbey

Westminster Abbey is where all British monarchs have been crowned since the coronation of William the Conqueror in 1066. Over 3,000 people are buried at Westminster, including many kings and queens, and writers and artists in Poet's Corner. One grave has no name on it: the grave of the Unknown Warrior contains the body of a soldier who died in France during the First World War. His tomb stands as a solemn reminder to all of the sacrifices made for one's country.

Big Ben

When people say 'Big Ben,' they usually mean the clock and tower at the end of the Houses of Parliament. But Big Ben is actually a nickname for the tower's largest bell. It is 2.2 metres (7 ½ feet) tall and 2.7 metres (9 feet) wide and weighs over 13 tonnes. Some say it was named after a beefy boxer; others say a chubby politician. Counting out the hours, Big Ben rings 156 times each day. That's a lot of bonging!

The London Eye

The London Eye is one of the largest observation wheels in the world. It was built to mark the year 2000 – a new century and millennium. Its 32 glass capsules can each hold 25 people. As they circle around, visitors can see up to 40 kilometres (25 miles), with amazing views of the Houses of Parliament, the dome of St Paul's and the jagged top of the Shard – London's tallest building. Originally, the plan was to keep the Eye for five years, but it proved so popular that it's now permanent.

The River Thames

London was once the largest port in the world. The River Thames, which joins the city to the sea, was busy with merchant and naval ships. Originally, the port activity was concentrated just downstream from London Bridge, in an area called the Pool of London. The Thames is Britain's longest river and also a tidal river. When the sea's high tide pushes its way upstream, the level of the river can rise by over 6 metres. That's the same height as a two-storey building!

Trafalgar Square

Trafalgar Square is a place for gatherings, demonstrations, celebrations, and a great picnic lunch. A tall column in the square holds a statue of Horatio Nelson, a British naval hero from the 1700s. His doctors said that when he lost his arm in battle, he was back to work in 30 minutes! He was killed in the Battle of Trafalgar at age 47. Look out for the Fourth Plinth, which holds no statue but has a changing display of artwork, such as a rocking horse or a huge blue rooster. What will it be when you visit?!

Hyde Park/Speaker's Corner

London has many beautiful parks, including Hyde Park, where a section is set apart for public speaking. The origin of Speakers' Corner dates back to 1866. Locked out of a government meeting, a group marched to Hyde Park, tore down the locked gates and rioted for three days. In following years, more groups protested in the same spot. In 1872, an act of Parliament set aside that corner as a place where anyone can speak, as long as the speech is lawful.

The Tube

There are many ways to get around London. One way is to ride the big network of trains that runs under the city. It's officially called the Underground, but most people call it the 'Tube', because of the shape of its tunnels. The Tube is the oldest underground railway in the world. In the 1860s, steam engines travelled the rails, but today's trains run on electricity. The Underground has 400 kilometres (250 miles) of track and 270 stations, and provides over a BILLION rides each year!

Rain

People often think that London is a very rainy city. It's true that skies are often cloudy, and each year over half a metre of rain falls on London. But that actually makes it drier than New York, Rome or Tokyo. Great Britain is an island, so weather changes often and quickly. Carry an umbrella – just in case!

Teatime

The custom of British afternoon tea may have begun in the early 1800s. It is said that the 7th Duchess of Bedford had a 'sinking feeling' between her morning and evening meals. Her solution? A nice pot of tea and a snack in the afternoon. She invited friends to join her and the practice spread. Afternoon tea is often served with tiny sandwiches, scones with clotted cream and jam, and sweet pastries. Yum!

Shopping
London is a great place to shop, with grand department stores like Harrods, Selfridges and Liberty. Busy shopping roads like Oxford Street and Regent Street have hundreds of stores to explore. For children, London has a wonderful array of stores for clothing, sweets and toys. Hamleys, the oldest and one of the largest toy stores in the world, is seven floors tall and has about 50,000 toys!

British Museum
The British Museum is the most popular attraction in London. Over five million people visit each year. The museum displays 80,000 objects, but owns over eight million! The Rosetta Stone, the key to understanding Egyptian picture-writing (hieroglyphs), is one of the Museum's most famous exhibits. Greek vases, Egyptian mummies, and precious clocks are among the other wonders to see.

St Paul's Cathedral
Before 1666, St Paul's was the tallest cathedral in England. But the Great Fire of London destroyed it and most of the city. Architect Sir Christopher Wren was asked to design a new cathedral. Construction took 36 years and the end result was a masterpiece. In fact, St Paul's is so beautiful that it has a 'protected view' – no new buildings can be built which would block its view from key spots in the city. When Christopher Wren died, he was buried in St Paul's. His tombstone reads: 'Reader, if you wish to see his memorial, look around you.'

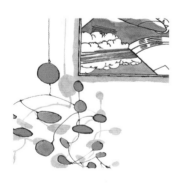

Tate Modern
When the Tate Gallery needed a place for its growing modern art collection, the Bankside Power Station was chosen for the project. The massive structure is made of over four million bricks and sports a tower 99 metres (325 feet) tall! Tate Modern displays art from Warhol, Picasso, Klee and Dali. The giant Turbine Hall displays a rotation of large works, such as a glowing sun under a mirrored ceiling, multi-storey steel and fibreglass slides and 100 million porcelain sunflower seeds.

The Globe
William Shakespeare was a famous playwright and actor, and a part-owner of the Globe. Some of his finest works, like *Hamlet* and *Macbeth*, were first performed there. The original Globe Theatre opened in 1599. In 1642 civil war broke out and all theatres were closed by government decree, so in 1644 the Globe was demolished. But in 1997 the rebuilt Globe opened – constructed from English oak, brick, and plaster – to introduce Shakespeare to millions.

Tower Bridge

Tower Bridge is a beautiful stone and steel bridge, built in the Victorian era. About 500 times per year, its middle part raises up to let tall ships pass through. Many people mistakenly call Tower Bridge by the wrong name: London Bridge. There is a relatively new London Bridge in the city, just west of Tower Bridge. An older version of London Bridge was sinking when it was sold to an American man in 1968. He took it apart, shipped it to the United States and reassembled it at Lake Havasu City in Arizona. So there's a little piece of London in the desert!

The Tower of London

After William the Conqueror invaded England in 1066, he built a huge White Tower on the Thames. Over time, other kings added more buildings and walls. The Tower of London has been a fortress, a prison, a royal mint where British coins were made, an armoury for weapons, and a place to keep jewels safe. The Tower is watched over by 35 Yeoman Warders, or Beefeaters, who live there. Every night, at exactly 9:52 pm, the Chief Warder begins his rounds in a ritual called The Ceremony of the Keys. Challenged by a sentry, he shows the royal keys and is allowed to continue, until he secures everything for the night.

Ravens

A flock of ravens lives at the Tower of London. Legend says that, should the ravens leave, both the Tower and the Kingdom will fall. A Yeoman Warder, called the 'Ravenmaster', is charged with caring for them. Every day, he feeds them meat, blood-soaked biscuits and other food. He keeps their wings trimmed so they won't fly off. At night, he secures them in special boxes to protect them from hungry foxes. Ravens like to steal shiny coins from visitors, so mind your pockets!